Facility Management for All

Jason Cousins

Facility Management for All © 2018 by Jason Cousins.

All Rights Reserved.

All rights reserved. No part of this book may be reproduced in any form or by any electronic or mechanical means including information storage and retrieval systems, without permission in writing from the author. The only exception is by a reviewer, who may quote short excerpts in a review.

Cover designed by Jason Cousins

First Printing: November 2018

Dedication

This book is dedicated to my
Camperdown High School
facility management
team for their untiring work
and my new grey hairs.

Table of Content

1. Thinking like a Facility Manager

2. Assess, Prevent or Pay
2.1 Water supply & drainage
2.2 Electrical and lighting
2.3 Heating, Ventilation and Air Conditioning (HVAC)
2.4 Sewerage
2.5 Building, grounds and security structures

3. Support the Support Staff
3.1 Assigning duties and tasks
3.2 Performance measurement
3.3 Team development
3.4 Conflict resolution skills
3.5 Taking disciplinary action

4. Oh Yeah! The Complaints

5. Controlling Creepy Crawlies!

6. Stop, Drop and Rollout a Safety Plan

7. Go Green, Save Green

8. Manage On!

Chapter 1

Thinking like a Facility Manager

Chances are you didn't just inherit a mansion in a will left by your secretly rich parents. Who thought it best to have you live a normal life and learn important life

values such as hard work and good financial management. You're not alone. There's a good chance however that you're a homeowner. Or you just opened your own business or landed a job in

real estate. In any case, you have a facility to manage.

Facility management like any other management discipline contributes to the overall functioning of an organization and the achievement of set goals. This may sound a bit business-like but think about it this way as well. If the roof of a family home, the facility, goes bad and starts to leak when it rains. Then the facility manager, mom or dad, has the responsibility to get this corrected so the set goal, living comfortably, can be achieved. Simply put, any physical structure whose walls are the scenes of activity needs management. Management that will achieve and maintain a comfortable living, working or recreating environment.

A facility's physical features, mechanical components, and their subsequent management needs are determined primarily by two categorical factors; meeting the needs of those occupying and operating in it and the ensuing wear and tear of their activities. The level of demand your job as the facility's manager will have on you is largely dependent on this level of traffic, activity, and wear and tear. For example, the level of traffic and wear tear that may be seen in an educational institution such as a high school will differ greatly from that seen in a small apartment complex. Other factors which are usually taken into consideration include environmental factors and its location. Fireplaces and heating systems are largely seen in areas with frigid climates such as Canada, northern United State or the UK. While states such as California, Florida or countries of the Caribbean depend greatly on efficiently operating cooling systems.

Besides these differences, there are ubiquitous features and elements to most operational facilities. These include:

- Water supply & drainage
- Electrical and lighting
- Heating, Ventilation and Air Conditioning (HVAC)
- Sewerage
- Building, grounds and security structures

The integrity and proper functioning of these systems will all contribute to an effective operational facility.

Chapter 2

Assess, Prevent or Pay

As the facility manager, it is your duty to know your facility inside out, where certain key areas are located and what normal function is like. If you're new to the facility, talk with maintenance team members, janitors and other key individuals who should be able to provide you with critical information about the facility's building structure and mechanical components. Ask about current issues relating to these and past attempts to rectify them. Seek to get diagrams of the facility's layout which may provide further information. As many mechanical and other components lie within walls and are not visible on a general walkthrough.

A general walkthrough assessment of the facility will allow you to have a big picture of your physical plant and help you to make better-informed decisions when making changes or responding to emergencies. The process involves taking a mental (or documented) note of normal functioning states. Colors seen, sounds heard, feel upon touch and even smells are factors you want to take note of. This becomes important upon initial problem assessment as oftentimes changes in these become telltale signs of dysfunction.

1.1 Water supply & drainage

A facility's water supply and drainage system take the precious commodity to all pipes, toilets, urinals, showers, and faucets within your facility. In all buildings, on all floors, and in all necessary rooms. Keeping this system in good working order means clean hands and a hygienic work or living environment.

Here are a few practical points and key areas to note:

- Find out where the main water supply and meter to your grounds/facility is located.

- Take note of where the branch water supplies enter each building or floor.

- Ascertain what type of pipes make up your plumbing system. Whether they be cast-iron. galvanized iron, cross-linked polyethylene (PEX), polyvinyl chloride (PVC), chlorinated polyvinyl chloride (CPVC) etc. The type of pipe used is often determined by the type of fluid which it carries. For example, PEX pipes may be used to carry both hot and cold water. While it is recommended that PVC and CPVC be used to carry only cold and hot water respectively.

- Examine the lock-off valves of the main and branch supplies for good working function.

- Locate each bathroom, kitchen or kitchenette, and laundry/wash area and examine each toilet, shower, urinal, facet, and pipe. Examine each for complete water stoppage when in the off position and a working lock-off valve for emergencies.

- Leave sink faucets and pipes running for a short period and examine drainage pipe for dripping and wetting on the floor beneath sinks.

- Examine flush handles and give the toilets a flush. Note the eventual stoppage of water entering bowl and proper tank filling which should end shortly after.

- Examine toilet inlet valves (usually located close to the floor behind toilet bowl) for proper functioning. It should stop tank filling when in the off position.

- Flush urinals and watch for proper emptying.

- Replace plastic flush handles with metal ones as they break less easily.

- Learn how to change a flush handle and replace toilet seat covers. Depending on the type of facility and traffic, you may need to do this every so often. Save money, do it yourself if you have to.

1.2 Electrical and lighting

Proper and appropriate lighting solutions are important and dependent on the type of facility, the area in which it is installed and the purpose it will serve. The type of luminaire (incandescent, LED, fluorescent etc.) used by different lighting fixtures will serve as the main determinant when choosing appropriate lighting solutions.

Here are a few practical points and key areas to note:

- Know the point where your main power supply enters your facility or grounds and the location of all electrical meters.

- Know where branch supplies enter each building or floor and the location of all relating electrical breaker panels.

- If not yet labeled, at an appropriate time, seek to identify what is controlled by each breaker unit by switching off each one by one and observing areas (both wall sockets and roof receptacles) for loss of power. Label breaker units accordingly (using a Sharpie and masking tape for example).

- Examine switches, receptacles, and sockets for broken or missing covers or corroding wires.

- Examine outdoor sockets for proper covering and weatherproofing.

- Ensure outdoor photocell (dusk to dawn) controlled lighting solutions are serviceable.

- Ensure there are no exposed, corroding or raw electrical wires on walls or ceiling.

- Learn how to change a bad switch, socket, and basic single bulb receptacle. It's easier than it looks. YouTube is a good place to start.

1.3 Heating, Ventilation and Air Conditioning (HVAC)

Consider this system the respiratory system of your facility. It ensures that each room on every floor is conducive for living or working. Of course, the components of this system will be dependent on the location of your facility and the corresponding needs for heating, cooling and air quality.

Here are a few practical points and key areas to note:

- Look for ceiling tile stains, water stains on walls, mold formation, and the condition of visible components such as thermostats and radiator valves.

- Pop up ceiling tiles and look through access panels. See if the ducts are insulated and check duct and pipe hangers. If there is a heat pump or fan coil system in the ceiling, see if tempered outdoor air ("primary air") is ducted to these units.

- For any equipment in the ceiling spaces, check condition, supports, and connections. For air conditioning units, check condensate drains.

- Inspect plumbing vent pipes and rooftop equipment such as makeup air units, air conditioning units, condensing units, and exhaust fans for leaks or disconnected pipes.

- Check components of the main mechanical or boiler room for leaking pipes, proper insulation, working relief valves and proper labels and up-to-date certificate tags.

- Check pumps for unusual noise and leaks.

- In examining each mechanical component, ensure they are properly fastened and anchor on roofs, walls, bases etc.

- Take note of thermostat and AC remote control settings under normal comfortable conditions (temperatures, mode, timer etc.) as a simple reset, restart or adjustment may get things running again.

1.4 Sewerage

The sewage system of a facility receives wastes from all bathrooms, laundry areas, and sinks. This particular system usually doesn't require much maintenance, but may lead to costly corrective measures if left neglected.

Onsite disposal systems utilize septic tanks which collect and store solid matter which have to be emptied periodically. These tanks possess leach drains which allow fluid to seep into the surrounding soil. Effluent wastewater systems, however, channel waste from the facility to a network of pipes connecting neighboring facilities in a municipal to a public lagoon. Often where it is treated.

Here are a few practical points and key areas to note:

- If not yet known, determine what type of sewage system your facility utilizes, whether it be an on-site septic disposal system or an effluent wastewater system.

- Ascertain whether your system is a gravity fed or a pump aided system.

- Locate all manholes making up your sewer network and ensure they are properly covered.

- At an appropriate time, open a manhole and make note of the type and size pipes making up your network. Gravity fed systems usual use PVC, vitrified clay pipes (VCP), high-density polyethylene (HDPE) or concrete pipes. While pump aided systems are usually made up of ductile iron (DIP), PVC, HDPE or Asbestos cement pipes.

- Weekly, pour a pot of boiling hot water down drains in kitchens and wash areas in two halves. Wait five minutes between. This removes grease build-up which may be lodged in drainage pipes.

- Each month purchase and treat your drainage pipes with an enzymatic cleaner. These bad boys are perfect for breaking down and removing organic matter. Ensure to use this when the traffic is the less heavy like after business operating hours or when the kids are off to bed.

1.5 Building, grounds and security structures

Your facility's physical structure houses all activities and requires much attention to details. Hazards are everywhere and can be virtually anything. As the facility manager, it is your duty to remain vigilant in order to correct changes in the facility's building and grounds which can become dangerous if left unattended to.

Here are a few practical points and key areas to note:
- Examine interior and exterior walls for cracks or any signs of disrepair.
- Examine window panes for breakages, cracks or missing blades.

- Check and ensure stairs, landings and handrails are in good repair and are fastened and secure.

- Examine doors for cracks secure hinges and door closers and working locks and bolts.

- Check all wood structures (ceiling, furniture, doors, cupboards etc.) For signs of termite damage. This is usually in the form of Smallwood grains on or in items or on the surrounding ground.

- Examine walkways, sidewalks, driveways and retaining walls to ensure they are in good condition and are free from trip hazards, cracks, and potholes.

- Examine decks and porches for cracks and loose or missing pieces.

- Examine perimeter fencing for signs of disrepair and possible sites for an intrusion.

- Examine barbed wire, spikes and other perimeter security structures for loose wires or missing spikes.

- Ensure gates are in good working order.

- Ensure the address gate number is visible.

- Examine signage and poles for loose screws and that they are securely fastened in ground or base.

- Examine security posts and ensure it's in good order and that lift arm gates are secure.

Ultimately, getting to know your facility will take time and much incidences of things going wrong. It will take time for you to know what you are able to correct yourself or when it's a job for the experts. However, one thing is sure, you will learn something new about your facility each time and gain an opportunity to prevent recurrence.

Chapter 3

Support the Support Staff

The scope of facility management involves the day-to-day facility upkeep activities to sporadic repair needs, weekly and monthly preventative measures to yearly  statutory inspections. Depending on the type of facility and resources available, you may have a team of persons which help you to carry out these functions. These persons may be directly employed by you or your organization or maybe a pool of individuals which are available to you when the need arises.

In either case, it is your responsibility to support (manage) these individuals effectively to keep your facility operating in such a manner that the organization's (or the home's) core functions are carried out efficiently. These individuals go by different names but primarily include custodians, cleaners, janitors, pool boys, gardeners, handymen, caretakers or watchmen etc.

Other maintenance personnel which may not be directly employed by you or your organization but whose services you will require include electricians, plumbers, refrigeration and heating specialists, carpenters, landscapers, welders, and locksmiths. It will prove worthwhile to keep a small directory of contacts for these individuals close. Also, seek to make friends with contacts at your local electrical, water, garbage collection utility suppliers as well as your local hardware. Introduce yourself and where you live or manage. You're going to need that contact in the future.

If you are new to a facility with an established support staff, one goal you may want to have is to earn their respect and one sure way to do this is to seek their input, thoughts, and advice. This is most effective when the individual is carrying out a task. In a manner willing to be thought, ask them about what they are doing. Why they are using the tools they are? How often they do it? Questions that will give them an opportunity to impart some knowledge to you. It shows your interest and respect for their work and contribution to the team. People like to know they have imparted knowledge to another person (especially their superior) just as much as people hate a know-it-all. They also like to know their efforts to impart this knowledge is regarded so ensure to listen carefully and apply when necessary. If changes have to be made or you have to decline their suggestions or opinions, respectfully communicate the reasons for.

Another sure way to gain your team's respect is to roll up your sleeves from time-to-time, depending on the task of course. There's something about becoming physically involved that makes the team see their superior in a one-of-us kind of light and thins a stick-it-to-the-man mentality which is often found among frontline support staff personnel. This approach, however, has to be balanced with a strict disciplinary structure proposed later.

Supporting this team also involves you ensuring they are equipped with all the necessary tools. You'd be surprised how the right tools make the biggest tasks easier and reduce downtime.

3.1 Assigning duties and tasks

Ensure to examine the requirements of a task carefully and that clear and detailed responsibilities are communicated when assigning these duties. Ensure that physical area, scheduled time and expected results are clearly defined.

Take into consideration the age, temperament, physical capabilities and experience of the individual when assigning duties. The youngest and strongest team member is oftentimes not the wisest choice for every duty. Especially when technical knowledge is needed. In this case, a more senior and experienced individual may be suitable.

Will the task involve some level of customer interaction or a great degree of physical exertion? Does the task require a special skill set or expertise? Does the individual require much supervision and instructing or are they able to work off their own initiative with minimal supervision? Considering such questions will help you assign the right person to get the job done most efficiently.

3.2 Performance motivation and measurement

When duties and responsibilities are clearly defined and communicated, it creates a system whereby performance can be measured against expected results. One of the greatest motivators for performance is knowing that tasks carried out may be assessed systematically or randomly. The truth is, at the bare minimum, individuals do what they know they will be inspected for. This provides a starting point from where performance assessment may be carried out. The key to such a system is to ensure this assessment actually takes place consistently and that constructive feedback, recognition, and reward are given or when necessary, corrective or disciplinary measures are taken.

3.3 Team development

Even if a team consists of just two persons, there are enough differences between the two that make direct efforts to develop a productive working relationship necessary. It is important that you as the facility's manager look at each member as a complex individual with diverse backgrounds and help them identify professional weaknesses. It is important to do so, as individual weaknesses ultimately lead to weaknesses within your team. This will take time, but adequately worked on, it will produce consistently optimum team performance. The use of team building exercises and activities are a good way to practically demonstrate how these may impact the team and how they may be improved. There are many resources available online or activity demonstrations on YouTube you may make use of free of cost.

Remember also that your team members are social beings with families, cares and lives beyond the walls of your facility. Engage them in private discussions periodically about happenings in their lives. Recognize and celebrate birthdays, anniversaries, outstanding performances, long-standing service, and other milestones. You'll be amazed how much of a boaster this may be to members of your team.

3.4 Conflict resolution skills

Conflict resolution is another art you will have to master as a supervising facility manager. It draws upon one's ability to remain neutral while negotiating to resolve an issue. The issue may be relating to virtually anything, but the principles of conflict resolution are practical and applicable to any problem that may arise. A key factor as the mediator in the process is to remain objective and impartial as you seek to resolve the issue. Seek to get to the bottom of the problem by asking relevant questions to ascertain a complete and detailed picture. When, how, where, who are the persons involved, what were the events leading to, what happened after, is the incident relating to a possible past unresolved conflict, how did you feel and what was your response are some of the details you may seek to acquire when discussing the problem with the conflicting parties.

Again, remaining neutral, begin soliciting possible solutions from them as a way to move forward and discuss together the feasibility of each suggestion given. In most cases, both parties will never become completely pleased but the ultimate aim of conflict resolution is to arrive at a compromise which both parties agree to and that will facilitate the effective functioning of the team.

The discussion process oftentimes also highlight possible workplace code of conduct breaches or basic unprofessional behavior. In such cases, you may be forced to carry out disciplinary action. Ensure that the parties involved are clear on what these are and your reasons for taking such action.

3.5 Taking disciplinary action

Most organizations usually have a set policy on taking disciplinary action when employees get out of line. As the facility manager, it's important that you find out these guidelines and adhere to them as closely as possible. If there is however not an established policy in place, a general rule of thumb is to start with two or three verbal discussions or warning regarding an occurrence. This is usually followed by documented reports and consequences to your discretion.

Chapter 4

Oh Yeah! The Complaints

There are no perfect facilities and inevitably things go bad. This may be due to constant wear and tear and many things even if left unused for long periods

become defective and require changing or servicing. With this background and depending on the type of facility, complaints are a sure thing. Though the word oftentimes evokes a sense of annoyance to the regular person, it's important that as the facility manager you begin the see them as a tool to help you better manage your facility.

Oftentimes what may be seen as a small complaint actually turn out to become the starting point of a larger more costly problem to correct and may have been avoided if attended to at the initial receipt of the complaint. Look at it this way, you only have two eyes and cannot be everywhere and take notice of everything but complaints help you to receive the necessary information about what is happening within various areas of your facility.

If you are new to the facility, take the time to visit the different areas be it apartments, departments, floors etc. and introduce yourself and your role as the facility manager. Become acquainted with those in charge of these areas and share some means of contact for you such as an established facility management department phone line or extension or a cellular number. Enquire if there are existing problems and what has been the results of attempts to rectify them in the past. Encourage members of your team to remain vigilant for problems and to inform you of these as they traverse these areas to carrying out day-to-day tasks.

Ideally, as the facility manager, you would want to correct every issue as they arise, but this is never always the case, as rectifying many problems require human, financial and other resources that are not always immediately available. Depending on the type of facility and the traffic, wear and tear may be greater and complaints more frequent. In this case, keeping a log of issues reported to you is a great way of ensuring nothing is overlooked. If there is something hindering a problem from being corrected, make notes of this so they may be addressed as soon as possible. In your log, ensure to also record the date of the complaint, who made it and when it was corrected as soon as it is.

Chapter 5

Controlling Creepy Crawlies!

In general sense roaches, rodents and insects go where they are attracted and remain there when they're allowed. Your ultimate aim as the facility manager is to reduce these attractions as much as possible and to maintain a clean and healthy working or living environment. The truth is, pest control within a facility is everyone's business and involves a general understanding of cleanliness practices among all who operate within its walls. It's your job as the facility manager to educate all on basic practices which will foster a healthy physical environment.

Here are some tips on effective pest control:
- Insist on immediate and thorough cleaning and sanitation of areas where food is prepared to include cooking grease and oils once complete and avoid leaving overnight. You'd be amazed how quickly this can attract unwanted company.

- Ensure there are sufficient garbage receptacles throughout the facility and make use of garbage bags which help your bins remain clean and odor free as possible. Use animal-proof garbage bins and ensure they are washed periodically.

- Keep cupboards, creases, and crevasses clean and dry by removing unnecessary storage and make use of shelves for neat and tidy storage.

- Limit the use of cardboard boxes for storage or change them regularly as they tend to attract cockroaches and rodents which feed on them in times of desperation. Use plastic containers instead. They are longer lasting, tighter sealed and do not deteriorate if they become wet.

- Avoid storing newspapers, magazines, documents and paper bags for long periods of time

- Prevent water from settling by fixing leaky plumbing, and do not let water accumulate anywhere in or around your facility. Do not leave any water in trays under houseplants, refrigerator, or in buckets overnight. Remove or dry out water damaged and wet materials as even dampness or high humidity can attract pests.

- Store your food in sealed glass or plastic containers, and keep your kitchen clean and free from cooking grease and oil. Do not leave food in pet bowls on the counter or floor for long periods of time. Put food scraps or refuse in tightly covered, animal-proof garbage cans, and empty your garbage frequently.

- Remove or block off indoor pest hiding places such as cracks and crevices to control pest access.

- Bathe pets regularly and wash any mats or surfaces they lie on to control fleas.

- Also, check for pests in packages or boxes before carrying them indoors.

- Block pest entryways. Install screens on all floor drains, windows, and doors to discourage crawling and flying pests from entering your home. Make sure any passageways through the floor are blocked. Place weather-stripping on doors and windows. Caulk and seal openings in walls. Keep doors shut when not in use.

- Remove or destroy outdoor pest hiding places. Remove piles of wood from under or around your facility to avoid attracting termites and carpenter ants.

- Destroy diseased plants, tree pruning, and fallen fruit that may harbor pests. Rake fallen leaves. Keep vegetation, shrubs, and wood mulch at least 18 inches away from your facility.

- Remove breeding sites. Clean up pet droppings as they attract flies that can spread bacteria. Do not accumulate litter or garbage; it draws mice, rats, and other rodents.

- Take proper care of all outdoor plants. These include flowers, fruit and shade trees, vegetable and other plants, and your lawn. Good plant health care reduces pest control needs— healthy plants resist pests better than do weak plants.

Chapter 6

Stop, Drop and Rollout a Safety Plan

Emergencies are a lot more manageable when planned for and planning for emergencies really doesn't take much. Many things can go wrong, hence  an emergency management plan is a comprehensive approach to minimizing the possibility of any eventualities and effectively responding to an occurrence to both preserve life and property.

The first step to developing a plan is to do a safety and emergency audit. Keep in mind that each facility has its own individual susceptible and safety needs and assessing your facility through an audit will tell you what are the things to get in place for your plan to be as effective as possible should an emergency arise.

Here are a few general considerations to take note of when conducting your audit:

- Take note of all emergency exists for all buildings and floors and ensure they are all clearly labeled according to national regulations.
- Take note of the location of all fire detectors and sprinklers and ensure they are in serviceable condition. Most modern systems have a test button installed for this purpose. Press and hold the button for a few seconds and a loud piercing sound or alarm should be heard. If this sound is weak or no sound is heard, replace the batteries and test again.
- Ensure each building, department or floor is equipped with a fire extinguisher that is in serviceable condition. Take note of key areas where uncontained fires are more likely and ensure these areas are duly equipped. Areas where open flames are lit regularly and are more likely to get out of control such as kitchens and kitchenettes. Also places with heavy electrical and mechanical equipment such as computer labs, electrical rooms, and basements as fires

are more likely to occur in these areas from an electrical shortage or lightning storm.

- If your organization is one with many floors, regulations may dictate the installation of wall water hydrants. Ensure these are in good working condition.

- Examine each outdoor water hydrant and ensure they are in good condition

- Examine emergency gates to ensure trucks may have easy access to the property.

- Ensure emergency outdoor meeting areas are clearly labeled.

- Create an emergency contact directory with numbers for your local fire, police,and medical services department and furnish this at key areas in each apartment, building, department or floor.

- Depending on the size of the facility, create several emergency exit maps of the entire property showing exit routes from key areas to emergency assembling points. It may be preferable to get this professionally.

Depending on the size of the facility and the number of individuals utilizing it, you may want to consider creating a safety and emergency response team. Members of the team could comprise members or heads of each apartment, building, department or floor. These individuals more than anyone else are equipped with occupational safety and emergency response knowledge and remain most vigilant. As the facility manager, you may spearhead this body and conduct regular training and sensitization activities such as how to effectively use a fire extinguisher, first responding, search and rescue and performing first aid activities.

Also, be sure to contact your local fire department and national emergency agency for updated recommendations for minimizing the risk of and responding to fires and earthquakes as well as preparing for and reducing the risk of property damage during hurricanes and flood

Chapter 7

Go green, Save green

Lately, making wiser choices and taking practical steps towards more sustainable living has become somewhat of a moral issue. Technology has afforded  facility managers the knowledge and tools needed to incorporate greener ways of living and working into everyday life and it's our responsibility to make use of these. The great thing about many of these recommendations is that they not only save on Earth's depleting resources but also help us save money, in many cases, big time!

Here are some practical energy saving tips:
- No matter what you've heard, LED is king! Tried tested and proven. Compared to other types of luminaries such as incandescent bulbs, LED bulbs provide great quality lighting for much less cost an oftentimes lasts longer. Seek to retrofit your lighting fixtures with LED bulbs.

- Retrofit refrigerators, air conditioning units and other cooling appliances with inverter models.

- Coat windows with low emissivity (Low-E) film. These work perfect for both winter and summer climate. During the summer it works by keeping the sun and ambient heat out and in winter it will work to reflect the radiant heat back into the room.

- Install insulation on exposed water heater pipes to reduce heat loss.

- Make use of energy smart power strips which turn off automatically when not in use.

- Utilize dust to dawn systems for your outdoor lighting. They turn on and off automatically with IR light from the sun, so you don't have to remember.

Here are some practical water conservation tips:

- Fix leaks as soon as you discover them. You'd be amazed as to how every drop add up

- Retrofit old toilets with newer ones which utilize less water for flushing. If this is not possible, retrofit toilets with tank banks which work by marginally displaces water so less fills with each flush. This adds up to a lot over time.

- Retrofit showerheads with low flow units, many of which provide a consistent flow of water regardless of water pressure.

- Retrofit faucets with aerators, small devices which incorporate air into your water stream to produce one constant flow regardless of water pressure. The volume of water coming from the tap is reduced resulting in savings.

Energy and water conservation involves everyone. As the facility manager, you may need to lead the charge in reminding those within your facility of this. Many small changes such as shutting down a computer at the end of the day or simply turning off the tap while brushing teeth can result in big savings.

Chapter 8

Manage On!

It is important to always remember that every facility is unique. Challenges that one may pose may be none existent in another. One thing is however sure, that as you rise to each challenge and overcome, you will learn something new, gain or strengthen a new skill and be convinced even more that anything can go wrong at any time. With a lifelong learning mind set, look at your facility as an adventure with each experience revealing something new about it.

Manage it well!

www.ingramcontent.com/pod-product-compliance
Lightning Source LLC
Chambersburg PA
CBHW040250220526
45473CB00001B/438